MW00738138

WORTHY OF HIS FALL

WORTHY OF HIS FALL

Poems by Richard Harrison

Wolsak and Wynn . Toronto

Cover Image: The cover image appears thanks to the Collection of the Glenbow Museum, Calgary, Canada, where it is catalogued and described as "MI-1863 A-B Kukri knife with tooled silver hilt and scabbard collar, ca. 1820. 12 fi inch blade."
Author's photograph: Lisa Rouleau
Typeset in Garamond, printed in Canada by
The Coach House Printing Company, Toronto, Ontario

The publishers gratefully acknowledge the support of the Canada Council for the Arts, the Ontario Arts Council and the Book Publishing IndustryDevelopment Program (BPIDP) for their financial assistance.

The Canada Council | Le Conseil des Arts
for the Arts | du Canada

Wolsak and Wynn Publishers Ltd
196 Spadina Avenue, Suite 303
Toronto, ON
Canada M5T 2C2
www.wolsakandwynn.ca

ONTARIO ARTS COUNCIL
CONSEIL DES ARTS DE L'ONTARIO

Canadä

Library and Archives Canada Cataloguing in Publication

Harrison, Richard, 1957-
    Worthy of his fall / Richard Harrison.

Poems.
ISBN 1-894987-04-7

    1. Fatherhood-Poetry. I. Title.

PS8565.A6573W67 2005   C811'.54   C2005-904481-0

For my father, Ralph Roland Harrison

CONTENTS

The day he tells me they've cut away his testicles
to treat his cancer, my father is an old man at the end
of the line. Miles away, I am a father, too, but my eyes
are my little boy eyes as my father lowers the mystery
of his scrotum into the bath with me, and the hot water,
rising, counts my ribs with its small hands:
this is how a man's body takes up the world
in the piling of water against white stone. This is
the body he has taught to me – and saved:
the pillar of his torso, arms and legs that sprung
the rhythm of his victories on the track,
crushing hands that played good cards and bad cards
always the same. And his voice, it hoisted any poem
up off the page. He is more island now than
ever in his soldier days when he learned to praise
the flesh that took a wound and lived, when
he built bridges out of range of enemy fire
and dropped them through the long stride of a triangle
onto the other shore. There he understood,
as he has always understood, the shortest distance
between mind and world is measured out in metal.
But my father is laughing on the phone
because the English learned to laugh
in the company of the dying and the dead. He will live,
we know it, because he has put his fighting laughter on.
He has let them open the folded purse where
the tiny machines that made half my body lay whirling
in the dark, and he quotes the Scrooge who found
his grave at the foot of his bed in the film my father
and I have watched every Christmas Eve I remember –
This, he is saying, *is not the man I was.*

11

He takes me with him to watch his ocean,
the waves replete with seabirds; beneath
the waves, he tells me, otters hunt.

All he wanted was his life in the army,
and no one who knew him
did not know that, too.

When I was a child, and he went to paint
the landscape, he wore his field coat into
the forests, the military green blending with
the leaves and shadows until he vanished into his art.

And when he came back home to us,
it was with the coat and canvasses
daubed in oils the colours
of every rock, branch and rapid he'd
looked at long enough to see.

He'd always spoken of purpose.
And patience, everything in order.
But today he turns to me with

the missing hours of his soldier's life,
and he offers their account while we walk
side by side, and the swimmers we have
waited for come ashore.

In honour of his father's lungs, Robert Hilles
and I lit the fat fingers of two Cuban cigars
in the only bar we could in downtown Calgary.
We summoned each puff, hauling
his father's hazy death into our chests,
and each of us knew in his own way
this was a celebration and a dare.
When my father tells me that his
was an anger that would have killed a man
with his naked hands had he not been stopped
(and he holds them out like a Buddhist monk blessing
those who fill his bowl with rice) I understand
Robert's desire to go into the burnt-out end
of his father's smoking days.
It was Nietzsche who said, "When you stare
into the abyss, the abyss stares into you."

Don't cross me today. I am hunting
for your disrespect. I feel a man's throat
in my grip, the need to set the fire
that consumed my Dad, and become worthy
of his fall.

My father's hands, spread out around the landscape:
see how the light shines off the hoods of cars, see
how women walk into caresses on the street.

My father spread his hands as if, in their posture,
they could find forgiveness for their presence
on another man's neck, the way they pressed
that man down and his feet drummed the ground as
my father squeezed the air from his throat.

This was 60 years ago, and it isn't the deaths
he caused because it was war and his job
that haunt him in the telling.

I remember my father by his wardrobe, its dark door
open. In the shadows his many suits kept watch,
and on the floor asleep lay shoes so loved
he wouldn't trust anything but the kiss of his own spit
to gloss them for the day, the way he'd learned
among soldiers, the way he taught me.

I remember him reaching in, returning
with a *khukri* laid across his hands –
the Gurkha knife hooked like a sword half-bent
to a ploughshare, and only the more deadly for that:

This was their fighting knife, he said.
This was his honour in their goodbye,
their gift to him notched at the hilt
where the priest had let the sacred in.
You could cut through a man's wrist
with a single, expert stroke.

My downfall, he tells me, *was I couldn't walk away.
I couldn't let him call me* yellow *in front of the troops
in the mess hall.*

Since I've come back from seeing him,
I haven't raised my voice.
I'm under control in a new way. I'm different.
I remember my father striking me as a child,
not hard compared to all he could have done,

but there's a sound you hear when it's your own head,
a clap of thunder at exactly the moment of lightning,
a heavy book dropped from the bed, that terrible Awake.

LOVE POEM FOR MY FATHER

You could see it the way his female
students gathered around him after class,
his gentle touch on their shoulders;
the way he'd pause in a sentence,
looking to the left and up – *listening,*
(if you were in love with him then, you'd have
said this was the pose of a prophet) and he'd
cup the room in his hand, weighing us
while we waited for the next word to arrive;
the way he'd coil his torso and
hurl a ball across the schoolyard:
It's not about strength, he'd tell us,
It's about timing.
He looked good in tennis whites.
His hair stayed dark until he was 60,
except the back of his head limned with silver
when he was 16 as if he always stood in the light.
His lips were tight with purpose as if
purpose were a clarinet, his cheek drumskin
smooth. When he recited his favourite poems,
a small stone jumped at the bottom of a shell.

I have replayed every furious scene with you.
That's a lie. There were too many.
They form one thing, the way a crowd
of houses and hotels springs up, and
suddenly, there's a city!
In the privacy of his home, a man throws
a punch at his bedroom door – for what
he can't remember – or watches
his two-year-old son holler without
shame because a brick of Lego won't grip
the dimpled foundation of his tower.
The man knows those fierce fists,
the scream that pierces like a whistle
affixed to a descending bomb, the eyes
that see nothing but the rushing air.
He comforts himself: *We are all like this
going in*, he says. But he knows that, too,
is a lie. He knows he has always cradled
this blinding rage. He's felt it flood
out of the father he loves, the father
of his doubt, the father of his silence,
the father of his tongue. *My God
is a difficult God*, he's told himself,
and he knows if he does not stop,
his life will teach his boy the old lie,
The beginning of wisdom is fear of the Lord.

My daughter adds her own lyrics
to a song of all things
missing their essential parts
like a fork without the appetite.

"Like a guitar without the string," I write
everything down I can knowing how
rare such words are that come to her
like visitors she will not remember,
and how the world,

like a garbage can – without the habit
has no way to catch and hold a child's art
except by accident. She's eight,

the age Plath was when her father
disappeared into the statue of himself
she spent her sweat and ink rebuilding
only to topple again and again
into a pile of mortar and blocks. Take note:

Every father has felt the dust of
chiseled stone settle in the hairs of his arms
as he labours under the gaze of his offspring.

My daughter greets me from the landing
when I come home from the blackboard;
eye to eye she leaps with faith
into my arms
        and her kiss hello.

I will be no Colossus, I say,
cast into a figure imagined or remembered
when the horizon is the floor.

And yet, as Emma nears
the heart and end of her verses,
her voice calls out *like*
a balloon without the helium:

Like a father without the yell.

Even in this hour come inklings of
the usual day, when I think of the
first stitches in my toddler's chin,
how I kissed my wife's lips as
I left for work this morning; in class
this afternoon, those of us over 40
went back through the times we had
lived out loud & I remembered
the Missile Crisis when I was sent
home from kindergarten with a note
to make my mother weep and sign
me away to safety – as if you could
ever find such a place on the earth.
And all we believed immutable
trembled in the bulkheads of
civilian planes flown into the
triumphant towers of the modern
world. And the towers collapsed
inwards like living things dying
the way Orwell wrote of the
elephant he'd shot breathing out
the mass of its life like smoke.
A week ago my daughter's godmother
dined atop an obelisk looking South
over the kingdom of New York;
yesterday a postcard arrived
with the Statue of Liberty
shouldering the moon. Even today

the normal day glanced up
when I talked with my students,
each of them as unfinished and
immortal as the wrongly dead who
live forever between beginning and
future and their unanswered desire
to know. And puzzled, they
just looked at us who'd lived this
long from the other side of the
glass of memory, and looking back
at their beautiful faces, I saw we are
all born unscarred.

WATER BIRTH
for Keeghan

With neither language nor a cry, you made me your father
The day you were born in a kiddie pool in our living room, and
You slid, calm as silver, beneath the surface of the water.

And they were green the way green trees bend toward the river,
Your mother, sister, the women around us crying out, reaching, as
With neither language nor a cry, you made me your father.

If I revere you here, it is a warning against my size, so revere
You I will: I whispered, *Like a god* of your face that flattened moment
You slid, calm as silver, beneath the surface of the water.

Then you did not know what you did *not* breathe was air,
For you were made full in a place without questions.
With neither language nor a cry, you made me your father.

And when they lay your blood across my scissors,
I swung the hinge on the door between your last life and this where
You slid, calm as silver, beneath the surface of the water.

You sit under the wind of this dry country like a settler,
in a chair made just your size in the room where you were born.
With neither language nor a cry, you made me your father.
You slid, calm as silver, beneath the surface of the water.

AN INNOCENT TO PRAIRIE LIFE SURVEYS HIS GARDEN AND
THE GARDENS OF HIS NEIGHBORS AFTER A HAILSTORM IN
JULY

There's nothing in the way things used to be
to tell him how to speak of this –
Like the garden's been put through a paper shredder? No,
that misses the water up to your shins, the hailstone lake
over grass in its prime, pelted leaves, their hands out for light
caught in the debris and ashes of an iceberg
exploded overhead. What single phrase for that?

For a time he wants a God, if only
to have someone to blame for broken skins on the vine –
roofs you can repair – and the devil will not do,
for he wants remorse as well
to float down and bless the shattered
heads of the nasturtiums his wife tucked
close in their bed, and of which his daughter
once said, *They look like people watching a movie.*

A half an hour and it's done. He gathers up
two handfuls of mealing slush, pitches
a snowball in mid-summer against a fence –
What else could he do?
This never happened back home where
the city congratulated itself everywhere you looked,
and he thought it a tribute to his civilization
and the wisdom of its leaders that his gardens
flowered every season and bore fruit.

The floor of the holding chamber in the slave castle
I stood in a decade ago on the coast of Ghana
is made of shit. Six feet of it, or more,
shit and every other effluent the human body
can discharge. You'd think it would smell.
But it doesn't. Left long enough in the heat,
tamped down by enough feet for
enough years, if you didn't know,
you'd say it was dry mud, like a country
road back home, or the walls
of a simple house built just outside
to fit the landscape and the weather.
But it's shit. And the only windows
in a room that held hundreds of people at once
are two holes cut into the wall, round and
desperate like the nostrils of a swimming pig
at the farthest corner from the door.
In the dark you understand at last
that these openings no bigger than your face
are only *now* head-high as you
measure a history four centuries thick
against the reach of your own small skin.
The guide will tell you the ones
who waited here sometimes waited half a year
to be funnelled one by one through the gullet
of stone to the Door of No Return, to
the big-bellied ships and the chains of the sea.

You reach down, touch the floor & realize
there is no honour you can give this place.
For that we have each other & words we never write.
For that we have holy books whose words remain
& for us to change in the reading. For that
they clean and repaint this castle: from the sea
it is white and spare like bleached linen,
and every week they dance along the walls,
singing in the night with their children
as if what happened here
was the happiest birth in the world.

takes Keeghan for a walk so the evening air can help him sleep, tells of the other grown-ups waiting at home with a game of cards and all the rums & cokes I'll need to soothe the pain of losing. It's about how, walking with my son, I stop and turn to look at a little canal with its spinning daisies and wildflowers in the wind, how the sun is setting & I'm disappointed with the Epilogue to *War and Peace*. There Tolstoy gives up on the novel, and he writes a 40-page essay on all that he believes. I feel betrayed. In the Preface, Leo said if he had a choice between writing a novel that would please and one that made his philosophies clear, he'd choose the first, and give not one moment's labour to the second. But then, in the way men so often are with choices, he tried to take them both. Still, in the epilogue, he says this: *the movement of the soul is as undetectable to our science as the movement of the earth is to our senses.* It's no real argument for the soul, of course – or faith – but it gives those who have faith a way to speak of it, and those who don't a chance to see what they miss. The sun is going down & the brain inside my boy is filling with a world where artifact and nature are one. He's looking at the daisies and the wildflowers spinning in the little valley the way I watch sports, and, holding him, I want to feel the earth as it tips the horizon up.

My son's penis disturbs me.
I wince when I see his open diaper,
or his baby hand reach down and pull
the tiny sock of skin untouched by metal
where mine was split and bared
for cleanliness' sake and looking
like my dad. It was the 50s when I was
born and everyone got cut,
but more than that, his penis says my own
is made around a wound. Yet still I cannot *not*
see the beauty I have spent so long to learn there;
once I read a poem by Sharon Olds who
saw in the rising head the kind of faithful
gentleness she observed as a child in the upraising
antennae of the garden slugs she used to watch, amazed.
And I wanted someone to see me emergent
and trusting. I've read more poems since then:
I know the image is more than the eye's desire:
the erection she saw was unsheathing
itself from the folds it was born with, in the way
nature protects its own; the tongue,
despite its strength, hunkers down behind
a gate of polished stones, the heart keeps its fire inside
an ivory lantern, the sweet devices of the ear
chirrup in the hollows of a scallop shell
deep beneath the poundage of the sea.

Keeghan, here is your body without artifact;
when you unfold yourself before another,
may you not be seen history first,
but with the beauty of my kind
and greater than my own.

KEEGHAN AND THE GREEN KNIGHT

Dear Keeghan, dear dragon, sleep sound.
You've fought off an illness even the doctors couldn't
name. And it cost you. There's a bruise
growing across your skull the way
spilled wine grows under cloth.
When it dries, it will take the shape of a dagger
pointing to the middle of your brow. Here,
you hammered your head against the end of your crib
as though what twisted in your bones
all night had used it as a shield.
And we, who loved you most, who tried
to place our hands between your body and
the relentless wood, could not make you turn away.
Tonight I see my son anew. You have been a knight
with a purpose; acted without question or
self-doubt, and there is something here
I have never seen before about the simplicity of honour.
I say the future has changed the past, even the past
of legend which is held to be eternal. From now on
this is how I will tell it: when he returns to Arthur's court,
having been spared by the Green Knight because
he kept his word and knelt to receive the blow,
Sir Gawain does not come back unmarked:
instead I will say, for the rest of his life
he carried the shadow of a blade where
the sword that could have been
his death brushed his neck lightly and but once.

1.

After a summer rain, my boy calls
from the stroller: *bho!* his word for *bird,* pointing –
three young robins at slaughter

2.

Aspen leaves in the breeze –
how they stop shining
plucked by his hand

3.

If you carry a baby,
people forgive you
for waving at the passing train

THE MARGARET LAURENCE I CAN TELL YOU I KNEW

The Margaret Laurence I can tell you I knew
slammed down the phone on the reporter digging for
a quote on "Gabrielle Roy's contribution
to Canadian life" while Gabrielle Roy lay dying.

The Margaret Laurence I can tell you I knew
didn't eat the dinner in her honour before her reading
at the University, read from trembling pages,
and afterwards was famished
when everything on campus was closed.

She kissed me goodbye after each of our conversations
at her famous kitchen table in Lakefield, Ontario,
but if I had asked her where to get published after the first one,
she'd never have talked to me again. We never fought.

The Margaret Laurence I *can't* tell you I knew
carried her cancer in her mouth, never healed
after the attacks on her books by the Christian Right,
did and did not believe *The Diviners* was her final novel.

The Margaret Laurence I can't tell you I knew
heard my voice among those who shared the particulars
of her final months, told me she had decided to die
on her own terms in a simple cup of coffee.

We never fought, and I let her down,
the Margaret I knew and did not know,
knowing only what someone could ever know,
too much in awe and eager to please the famous.

AN ELEGY FOR TIFF, A POEM FOR BILL
for Bill Whitehead and in memory of Timothy Findley

When we talked together at Margaret Laurence's memorial
in the Great Hall beside the Otonabee, I said, 'She took me in
as one of her *Tribe*. For the rest of my life, I'll owe her that.'
Tiff turned to me, half-turned, the way a man checks
his truths in the back pocket of his eye, and said,
'Oh, many of us owe her *that*.' We were young men in those
days sheltered by her shadow. He didn't need to speak that way –
he'd already published shadow enough to put his own arm
between a sky of critical hawks and a writer thirty years his junior,
and I'd have never seen the difference. But watch the best actors
at their work – they who support both stars and bit players
with a single line. I was hanging a blind across a window
the night I heard the news; when it was done,
I raised it like a curtain on the dark. The nation grieves for Tiff,
who flattered it with his beauty and stung it with his tongue,
a combination butterfly and mosquito, who received
the country's love and loved it back like a suitor
not yet one of the family, who took in poisons
and ambrosias together because he knew
the world is a pagan thing to be consumed precisely as
it comes with a smoky, fearless laugh and an eye cold full with fact.
But you knew best how uneasy his love was, how,
like a broad river it tumbled the stones in its bed;
how he could lose himself in *Timothy Findley*
the way a king might be lost in the corridors
he builds in the castle of his fathers.

Those who loved him for his words loved only
the half a man a lighted page can let us see;
you loved him clear through
to all he had ever been from birth.

A SHORT STORY ABOUT STRING

I see it with the clarity we save
for all things lost –
the enamelled silver Thunderbird I bought
in a Native Craft Store (to use the language
of the time) in Toronto in the 70s.
As if I believed, I hung it from my neck
for every high school exam I faced.
Now I look back and see a thin white boy
tipping on his collarbone the sign of a religion
neither his own nor by his people loved:
That I lost the thing is undoubtedly right, I say,
choosing to say "undoubtedly right" because
Ray Souster taught that there are poems
incomplete without their makers' judgment
said out loud. Why mourn?
Because I miss the string, the double-loop
of leather around the ring at the Thunderbird head,
for when I bought the bird, the man
who owned the shop –
his name was John Sears and you
should know that too –
he took a patch of leather the size of my palm,
& smiling, said, *I can make you a string from this.*
Think you can tell me how? And when
I could not, he took a scissor
and cut the patch into a spiral,
twirling and massaging the leather
with his rig-worker hands.

In his homeland, north of the city
& surrounded by my government,
he was a carver.
If you are working on a carving, he told me,
and you're on the thumb, but
you keep looking to the ear,
go work on the ear.
And then the skin was done,
slender and fine. And I lost it.
Years later, long after I'd given up
on the bird and its leather umbilicus,
my daughter, beads in hand,
needed a string for her necklace.
Picking up a scrap of leather
from her box of pieces and cloth,
I said, *I can make you one from this.*
Think you can tell me how?
This would be a different story
if she couldn't. But she could.
She'd seen her grandmother do it
when she stayed with her last summer.
Still, you need grown-up hands
for the job. I unwound the string
from the little rag, turning it
where the leather met the blades
round and round in a narrowing gyre
while she watched me with her
knowing eyes.

Emma tells me I cannot count to one.
This is no insult. It's math. And she is
serious as a comedian about making something
happen in my mind. *Negative infinity,* she says,
is the lowest number in the negatives, right?

These days I'm working on puzzles of my own:
the green plastic chair on the balcony,
the blue balding head of an old magpie in the rain,
a red clay stone kicked from the boulevard: images.

And negative one is the highest.

OK.

No, even more basic and difficult: *the* image,
the *word* that *is* the thing: sensuous, experienced,
your mouth so full, you are deceived.
Think *mango. Tin Can. Brick.*

So if you start at negative infinity and go up,
you'll never get there, will you?

She's got me, and while
we are laughing, I look around the room
with an accurate measure at last
of the distance between words
and that pot of flowers on the table
I'd like you to see.

I love you, that much is always true
though they say that love burns low
the longer it's lived through.
I love you, that much is always true
when its light shines into the depth of you.
So they are wrong who do not know, through
"I love you, that much is always true,"
when love burns long that love burns low.

Last night I dreamed I was in bed with
my first wife in a small, wooden room.
She had worse teeth than I remember.
I think it's a sign. No one forgave anyone.
I need to forgive. Not just her, or me,
or those who saw us and said nothing
because those were the days when respect
meant leaving someone alone. If I could,
I'd travel back and say, *Richard,*
you're throwing your life away.
To which my younger self would reply,
*But I **love** her.* And to that I'd answer:
Coward.

The dream was full of small, dark rooms,
their images left from my trip to The Tunnels
of Moose Jaw, Saskatchewan, where
generations of men from China were robbed
of all the years they had ahead. Everyone
smug about Canada should walk through
those holes and burrows, see the photographs
of men who took a decade to climb
200 feet from the laundry
to the burlap factory under Main Street.

There are faces there to compare
with any in your life of men
full of story and small with words.
How can you make how fortunate you are
answer those raised eyebrows before the camera,
those silent chests?

THIS POEM IS NO PRAYER
in memory my great-uncle, Richard Albert Harrison, 1896-1915

You died in your war without ever moving over the battlefield,
swept from the scene by disease instead, the way more young
men were (though we forget) than ever were killed by metal.
All you have in our family's oral book is a story no longer than
a sentence. Yet I name you (as you named me) in a search for
faith, for myself among the disciples and a saviour breaking the
crust, saying, *This is my body – eat of me,* as he passes over into
the skin of the bread and the saved. Since the birth of my son,
my second child, I have let my tongue touch religious language
like a tooth suddenly peopled with nerve. This poem is no
prayer, but I begin and begin again with you dying in a room
the colour of a jar of olives, all your soldier's training unable to
raise the tent of your lungs even to make room for your dreams.
And I give you something in that moment that only you can see.

THE SCHOLARS PRESENT THEIR RECONSTRUCTION OF
THE REAL FACE OF JESUS, DECEMBER, 2002

If this *is* Him,
with the look of
an exhausted nose-tackle,
helmet pulled off,
hair full of heat,

then His is a face
only a few would love up close,
but many would love
from afar; I can see this man

parting the adult sea
to make way for the little children;
I can see him

tossing out the money-lenders
with an *And STAY out!*
worthy of Yosemite Sam.

I can see Him, uncultivated,
un-handsome, smoothing
my uncle's brow;

A good choice,
for I imagine the dying
hate the beautiful surface of things.

We can all raise the dead,
heal the sick, feed multitudes;
we can all speak in tongues
the way I heard them when I walked
into the church in Ghana,
the way *they* walked in
on the apostles in the Acts
and heard them babbling like the drunk.
And it *is* wettened speech,
how someone begins to talk
before putting down the glass,
a swimmer's mouth open
in the pool. I remember
the minister's sporty, sweating face,
the drum and the drum, the
dresses brilliant with lore and
story around the thickened women,
the voluptuous, the motherly,
we are all alone with God.
Each of us walks with Jesus
at a singular loss for words. For what
is language except names
for everything we've agreed to share?
What else could the spoken text of
every self-orbiting hallelujah *be* but *this* –
tumbling syllables meaning what
no outsider understands but those
who speak their untranslatable tongues
all do?

There's a poem in these two –
midway through their adolescence yet
stumping for the Lord beneath my lintel –
a poem beyond the easy connection between
them and the zealots who make the paper.
We live in an easy part of the world;
perhaps their God is just a God of
super-powers and ill-gotten plenty
mistaken for reward. These are not just
photographs of boys; they don't hold still
while I stare. The one who does the talking
swings the Bible in a little circle,
quoting without looking, so
it's not a book anymore, and
he uses it to emphasise the point
in the intimate way we gesture
with a sandwich in the lunchroom.
I know I know nothing so well.
I'd like a reason to close the door.
They almost give it to me when they say
they know why two girls, hiking
with their parents, died under a windblown tree
in a National Park – such conviction!
And consistent, too, with the plan of a God who
Himself went under the nail to fix our worship
to His Blood. But that's not it, and it isn't
what I see looking into my house –

two outsiders: *geeks, fags* in the language
of my publicly educated life, the kids who
embraced their books the other kids
hated all the way to the last years of High School
when marks meant University and jobs and I was
suddenly in demand for help.
That is what I will not see –
how odd, in the world of birth
and sickness and news of war my middle years
have become, that it's the time when I was them
I cannot bear in their foot soldiers' plea
to join them in their love.

POEM ON THE WORDS OF DEFENCE SECRETARY DONALD
RUMSFELD SPOKEN 40 DAYS BEFORE THE LAUNCH OF THE
U.S. WAR ON IRAQ

I knew a little thing like the border
wouldn't get in your way, Rumsfeld.
That's how you got into my bed
this morning with your coffee and the news,
snapping the pages like bad reception
in my ear. And sleepy as I was, I knew
it was you, peering down your high-powered
squint at the world's rejection of your argument
why tortured and child-heavy Iraq still
had weaponry to burn. You're a man
with a job to do and little time left,
and the U.S. was good to your kind
even before the ancient ex-Mariner with
your haircut came second on *Survivor* –
        but won America's heart.
Here, we're worried about
how little snow there's been again, how
little water the bare mountains mean
come spring, and the sun attacks
our thirsty food in the soil where
it's been sown. But you've had enough.
You turn the cross-hairs of your eyes
away from the words before you.
What I don't understand, you complain,
your mug steaming,
your jaw firm as a rifle's butt,

is this obsession with proof
beyond a reasonable doubt.
Then off you go.
Hey! Rumsfeld –
since you're out there making History,
let me put it in the grandest terms:
Nations are greater than individual men.
But each can fall in a single sentence.
Sometimes it's the one pronounced upon them.
Sometimes it's the one they utter themselves
from the trigger end of the gun.

This is a political poem, so
don't expect beauty, for
warnography sticks the camera in
where only blind organs
are meant to go: now you can see
soldiers moving in a green world
as if under water through the lens
of night-vision goggles in the
desert dark; warnography
lets you gaze down the shaft
of the cannon from your
privileged hips in the turret.
You can almost lick the skin
of the Stealth Bomber –
a plane so black & smooth &
shiny, it seems to be made of oil.
Just imagine what that baby's
gonna do. It's you
in the tip of the cruising missile
all the way to the score:
Baghdad Burns in the newsbox –
they're hot because you're watching
what's happening over there.
What you'll never get on
CBS, NBC & C-INANE
is Wilfred Owen's war. And

maybe a man drowning
in his own lungs *is* erotic
in the way that all that happens
to real flesh in the real world
won't let you sleep, but
it's bad TV. Last night
I got my first instalment
from a reporter perfectly coiffed
for battle from his position
"embedded" with the troops –
a little webcam bit from
Apache and *Bonecrusher*
Cavalry Battalions &
        the little men moved
in the primitive stop-action way
it used to be on *The Home Shopping
Network*, and I wanted to ask,
Does that artillery come in
cubic zirconia, or can I only
get it in a beige that
mocks the colour of biblical sand?
I'm mad. Of course I'm mad.
I'm mad that Osama bin Laden,
trained by the CIA,
using tactics as old as Troy
& the corporate structure of
a cosmetics giant

has been able to use the USA
to prove that those who forget history
can be forced to repeat it,
that George W. Bush has turned
the wheel that began to roll
with the assassination of the Kennedys
and King, and America, like Rome
before it, is no longer a Republic
but an Empire, and all the world
is divided into three parts.
I'm mad that this war will go on
a month longer than it has to
because there are missiles that need
to be buried for the Americans to find –
for warnography, like the literature of whores
still requires she deserved whatever she got.
I'm mad that my daughter, seeing
the bombardment, said, *I'd never surrender.*
And I said, *I would*
because, unlike an Iraqi father
tonight I can stop thinking about
my child's death;
I'm mad because I still see,
when I close my eyes & listen
to the bursts, the Eiffel Tower

lit up with fireworks to celebrate
the Millennium – a pillar of curving
light, a column in a church
built from the reflection of the moon.
But I should have known:
This is the 21st Century –
Don't expect beauty.

SADDAMANDIAS

I watched a soldier in an antique land
who set Old Glory on a statue's eyes
and cast down the bronze trunk from its stand
in the desert . . . Near him, despised
like junk, a shattered visage lies, whose frown
and wrinkled lip, and sneer of cold command,
could yet survive, in a sonnet blind to boundless
hearts stamped beneath the sand to lifeless things.
And on the pedestal I wish these words appeared:
"My name is Saddam Hussein, Pawn of Kings.
Look upon Your works, ye Mighty, and despair!"
But nothing of the kind remains. The decay
in that colossal wreck no sculptor bared,
nor mocked the hand that fed from far away.

I turn my back to the light I see through the blind,
to the colour green, to Cardinal Newman's sentence,
(quoted by William James): "pious as it is
to think of [God] while the pageant ... passes
by ... such piety is nothing more
than a poetry of thought, or an ornament
of language, a certain view of Nature,
which one man has and another has not."
Shall I pray because my friend's
son's cancer is in remission? Because
my father is alive? For peace?
Shall I pray because the curly forelocks
of the Caesars have grown on the brows
of America? or because, even though
the young men who threw a cream pie
in our Prime Minister's face were apprehended,
they will live the night?
Shall I pray *not* to see poor Hegel
use the word *real* in such a way
that if I used it to speak of things
knowable outside the language,
all the grad students would laugh out loud
and I'd get no more than a B?
Shall I say that real things happen
to people no one speaks of; shall I pray
for them, the unspoken of, as if
being anonymous and unrecorded
by others is a curse?

Jesus knew the evils of the Church to come,
choosing to found His house in the flawed arms
of Peter, stubborn Peter, fearful Peter, Peter who
betrayed Him, as Jesus knew he would,
denying Him every time he had the chance
before the proud rooster declared
the break of morning to his flock. Peter, who,
in so doing, *lived*, did his work,
and demanded to be crucified upside down,
not worthy of his Saviour's fall. I was raised
without belief, and have let the failings
of women and men cover the face of whatever God
there is and I deny (my desire for faith exceeds my faith),
and yet the story answers at least this
(consider how many versions it has survived):
if faith *is* the rose that blooms in the tended garden,
the Church, a human thing, is not its root,
reaching down for food, nor the sun
that perpetually offers; it is the part
that does what it must, all that's left of
those who suffered here. It is the shit,
the beautiful shit.

POEM IN MEMORY OF MY STUDENT, PROFESSOR RUTH MCKAY

Ruth, my kids just love The Calgary Tower.
That's why we were there the afternoon
your car rolled on the road to town
and Jim died at the scene. It's why
we saw the bright red air ambulance
with you inside fly like a flung heart
over the rooftops, and I remember saying,
There, kids, that's someone with a purpose,
while the rest of the city puttered on
higgledy-piggledy below the big windows
Keeghan leaned against to watch. For poetry,
there are no coincidences, only chances
to make meaning. The line of yours that
haunts me best is, "Today, I saw air" –
that line, and how surprised you were
at such a folly after 70 years, 3 grad degrees,
four children, two careers, the second
as professor; after a life devoted
to the practical world and the text,
how you laughed and looked to
Evelyn and Garda on either side of
you pleased as a bingo winner.
You knew you had it in you,
it's why you were with us, giving
yourself to writing the poem,
and dying, true to your faith,
beyond the bindings of any science,
any book.

Son of a bitch, that Jesus, every day
insisting on His existence, me not
believing yet unable to reason away
the empty room. I have knocked on
a door I do not see, and everything
I see tells me it is not enough.
Like Homer, I used to love the heroes
of strength, even down to the last sons &
daughters of envied Hercules whose name
means Superhero, thief of colour
and the muscles of men.
But no comic book could
open like a chapter in *The Odyssey,*
no novel like a Bible verse. No poem
can still this unease – that I must have
a Heaven for the dead whom I have loved.

to the unnamed soldier on the front page of The Globe & Mail
*shown receiving word that the U.S. will be extending his tour of duty in
Iraq – promised to be a few months at the outset of the war – for
"an indefinite period."*

The Bible says God sees the fall of even the humble sparrow –
this is the measure of His compassion. And I have always read Williams'
elegy as God's eye view of the bird. Then I saw your schoolboy face,
weary with the news. Today every poem is a war poem,
and your skin, the colour of the streets, becomes the effigy of itself.
This is your hair thickened with city sand like feathers
peeled from the road by small children. Some of you will die
when a citizen who never surrendered sees his shot
on an ordinary street. You know this. And I find your epitaph
in the poem: It is no trumpet blast. Nor will the authorities of
your trust, who put you in the way, their mouths marbled
with the lies of glory, be able to say it: *This was I, a sparrow/
I did my best. Farewell.*

Margaret loved the words
Lord, I believe. Help thou my unbelief!
and she, beset by those who believed too much,
found in the Bible's cry, broken
and set against itself, her mirror and her shield.

Her death surprised me, then it did not –
she, the most faithful believer who ever
taught me going blithely
to that promised heart and hiding place.

Almost daily, I dwell on the sentence, "No one
is more alone than one alone with God." I say
it is true and not true.

Consider Jesus in green Gethsemane, who brought
the Bible's Second Act to a close in the same place
Act One began – a garden and a man doubting himself.
Perhaps the Miracles were done to convince
Christ more than anyone else,
for doubt is boundless, and proves nothing.

MARCH 11, 2004
for Gilles Mossière

See how safe the world is now – what with
Saddam Hussein in custody, George
Junior his Triumph got:
al-Qaeda murders by the calendar
the way I host a birthday party for my son.
Gilles, my friend, colleague across the hall,
translator, last time I saw you, you were
celebrating the end of class with
the Spanish students from graduate school.
We were in the Ethiopian restaurant where
you go when your appetite's a well
you have hours to fill, and you want
the kind of service that reminds you
there are people in the world not living
every minute by the clock. Still, we chuckled,
didn't we? in our confident, North American way,
at how long it took the students to arrange
a skating party in the town square
(it never happened) or get the gang together
for one night's meal. The mouth of Spain
is filled with tears. On the soccer pitch,
the teams bear the nation's flag as if
to dress a coffin. On the colours is painted
that black ribbon that looks like a fish
drawn by a child, a question mark

bending its head towards a mirror. It's almost
Easter, and in his *Passion,* Mel Gibson is out
to prove that Jesus could take it,
daring the Romans, *Do Your Worst!*
And the American audiences gobble it up
because Christ's Yankees are tough guys, too –
like their Saviour, tough as nails. But
nobody chooses the God that made them,
nobody chooses who they are born foreign to;
every day people go about their business,
get on trains, go to work, go home,
and today a thousand innocents in Madrid
are covered every square inch with real blood
rendered by one Defender of the Faith
unto another in the unspeakable tongue of their kind.

You knew there would be more
the minute you saw the photographs
from the collection at Abu Ghraib,
Saddam's old cells still drawing breath
in American arms, but even then
what you saw reminded you
not of the torsos and chambers
you've toured in the wax museums
of history and the evening news,
but the footage you can find on the Net
under the search-words *amateur* and *sex*.
And those sites will tell you,
in the sincerest of fonts,
that the people exposed for witness there
are *real*, like you, meaning:
not actors; meaning: on consignment.
And behind the prisoners' hooded heads,
interlaced limbs, bare asses, the grins
on the faces of the guards are the grins
of men and women who know their porn;
they are fulfilling the Academy-Award-
winner's fantasy not just to act, but direct
as well, a dream he speaks of
with the gold swordsman
at attention in his arms and heavy as
a drawbridge key. In the village
square of television, the Commander-in-Chief

issues his executive apology, and blames
his secretary to make it complete.
Then the comedians come out from behind the drapes,
the jokers, hosts of talk shows who jest
that the politicians responsible
should prove their penance
with a naked human pyramid all their own.
And you watch as the audiences squirm
and giggle because the only thing
that turns them off more than
the thought of one old man filled with
sexual ambition is a whole bunch of them.
No one wants to see that – especially if
it's not coerced. There had to be more.
By now the stones of Abu Ghraib
have been scrubbed clean,
and soon the prison will be brought
to the dirt brick by brick for shame.
It may already be gone. But when
this war is tallied up at last,
may they count themselves
among the obscene, those
far away and safe at home
who laughed like the jailers who
forced men before a camera
and made them hump each other
at their feet.

ANYONE WHO MARCHES IS AN ARMY

When I told my father about parading
for peace with millions around the globe,
how I thought our point was only moral,
not advice against the U.S. starting a war
it couldn't win, and I laughed at the irony
of a peace march being correct
in military terms, he said,
Anyone who marches is an army.
It's a comment I've held on to
through every newscast and defeat
for the peace I thought could be found
at the end of a long group-walk or anthology
of pleas. Naïve? Perhaps. Surely –
But don't we have the vote?
"Anyone who marches is an army,"
he said from where his own war wrote
with an angry, childish hand in thick white ink
upon his skin. If he would but bless me now,
my fingers could read what lies un-gently
in the flesh of his silent remembering. He knows
what a man learns when he's unprepared
and too young, as the boys from Utah, or upstate
New York are unprepared and too young
for a people turned against them one by one.
Dad knew – he told me from the start,
*The Americans' mistake is they think they can
make friends,* and I read in his words that war
makes everyone a traitor given time.

It's true. There's a father on TV pointing
towards his bombed-out house. Still
and unbreathing, his children
lie buried beneath, and of all the terms
this man could choose to send his message
to what remains of the world as he passes
before its bottled eye, he chooses the political:
If this is democracy and freedom
the Americans bring, he says,
Why are my children dead?
Now we're in it, openly trading images
of a beheading in Baghdad, of prisoners
tortured – with promise of worse
at American hands. I imagine my father
in a different conversation,
one we've always understood
we'd never have between us: *Don't ask me,*
if you had the chance to do it again,
would you go? We were loyal
to our country, and those of us
who had one, to God. I know
you love this in me, but let me tell you,
bound by honour alone,
whole armies can be undone.

1934

God lost my father in 1934
when a boy went to see
his grandfather in the Invalid Hospital
in Leeds where there was nothing
for the working man's broken back
back then but patience and murmurs,
and a sight to blind you to every sign
of His professed love.

When my father had a heart attack
not long ago, he kept me
from his bedside till he could
raise himself again, and I have not
seen him yet. God,
my father is a difficult father,
to his own self true,
as he has always preached,
even to the last.

I confess, too, that I have been tempted
by prayer, despite the warnings,
and wanted the God of this page
to be the same
as the indifferent Father of a yawning heaven,

for God to be small as Jesus
before God took Him back
and placed Him beside Himself
where a son belongs,
or so it is written.

I wanted God in awe
of the latest photos from NASA
with *fifty galaxies* in a patch of sky
no bigger than a fingertip,
and God helpless to stop
every innocent death between the beginning
of this poem and now.

Only an impossible God like that
could open the eyes of my atheism
and relieve the great comfort
of the dark.

STATE[MENT] OF MY FAITH

If you asked me, I'd go down not believing.
That's pride, or a truth I haven't been afraid enough
to deny. Light is everywhere and
strange. Sometimes it bounces
off the bottom of an empty bowl
so that it seems to rise
from nowhere to the lip. The pharaohs
knew the sun and arranged to read
their sacred ceilings by God's light
in the tomb. I pray now;
once my daughter lay dying – or
so it might have been, and like a man,
say young Dostoyevsky, fit as a Russian fiddle,
awaiting execution with his sentence
commuted, the burden was lifted
from my blood. And to see her today,
you'd never know. My hope is more than hope
it will be lifted from the ones I hope for too.
And I would believe
in a spirit almost powerless before nature,
or the awkward facts of weakness and evil.
Imagine believing in Jesus but not
His faith, the earth cradled
in the nesting bowls of the sky
like a yolk armoured by its shell –
no more than the ancients imagined,
no more than the imagination requires
for wonder.

When my father saw the signs
that he might die if he did nothing,
and he might die anyway at that,
blood thickening in his stomach
like red wax poured in a cold cup,
he took a bath.
While the ambulance sang
to him from the streets,
he undressed and took a bath,
my father, alone and naked
in the water, ready for his heaven.

THE MOST DIFFICULT THING TO RENDER INTO ART IS YOUR
OWN FACE. BE HONEST.

Yesterday, while my son brushed his teeth, I looked in the mirror.
My glasses rode low on my nose. I needed a shave.
My God, I thought, kneeling to help my child finish the job,
*I've become **a father**.* That's no surprise. The surprise
was it was not *my* father I'd said to myself I'd become,
having spent years detecting every quirk and manner in
common to us both. The other day, my son asked,
Dad, were you ever a little boy? With a face like me?
And when I said *yes*, he laughed so hard,
he did a little back-flip on his bed. A nice story to sleep on.
Legend goes a man becomes his father and fathers a son in turn,
but that average, middle-aged man I saw with my boy that night,
he was no old warrior – if anything, he looked like the owner
of a bookstore who works too late too often. But I liked him, and,
to answer your question, I liked him beside you, helping you
with your teeth before bed. I know things. You will look for me, too,
in the face growing old I told you was once like mine.
But do not find me. You'll be a happy man.

Part of every day, I wait for my father to die.
This book waits with me, composing itself.
This book, like all books, casting its cold eyes
to the world made in its image.
It holds my hand, but it loves to close
as all books do. Even the Bible, that book of hope,
took down its entire readership just to finish.
Maybe my father will die while the book
is open. Or he'll escape and ready himself
on his own terms, and the book
will have to accept that life goes on without it,
defying the odds. Imagine Ahab risen from
the back of The White Whale, Hamlet only wounded,
and courageous at last from the wine.
Who am I kidding? It is we who rest in peace
on the last page, our need to see something
conclude the poison in the Prince's cup;
all literature is flattery, and what greater gift
can a book give than to say, *You are alive, dear reader,
sleep well.* My father is too weak for the surgery.
He needs to rest, walk more, eat more red meat.
And wait for the decision to be made for him
with the shining edge of a healing knife.
On the phone, he tells me of the weariness in his legs;
he asks me how the book is coming along.
I'm not fooling him. He knows this work,
preparing for the end when all we are is words,
words, and the silence when someone reading them
is done.

ENVOI

Dear Dad,

I have held your story like a juror with the murder weapon
in his palm who presumes the plastic bag will let him feel
the mass of guilt without the stain.

You did not ask to be forgiven, or put the mark of regret
upon my forehead, the weight of the missing world
fallen, at last, from your shoulders.

Against your teachings, I looked for God. It was natural, I'm told,
for those left alive by middle age in a country where, as one poet said,
there was never so much food.

Yet it has taken me until now to witness two births in my house,
and lower two coffins by a field where black cattle graze even in winter.

Don't worry. I didn't find Him, though I found words
for the longing when the world is made in His image.
In the cave between receiver and ear,

when all that's left of us is voice, I asked
why you told me, and I saw you, at last, as a man for whom
death was never the worst thing on his hands.

Here are my poems because you replied, *You had to know.*

NOTES

Some of the poems in this book, or earlier versions of them, have appeared in the journals *The Malahat Review*, *West Coast Line*, *filling station*, and *Alberta Views*, in Copper Canyon Press's electronic anthology *Poets Against the War*, in filling station's chapbook/calendar *Calendric*, and in the anthologies *Gifts: Poems for Parents*, and *The Edges of Time*, both from Sumach Press.

"Song for the Lesser Giant" had its origin in my daughter, Emma, singing the lines italicized in the poem. Later I discovered that these were her further improvisations on Kris Demeanor's "You're You," which she'd heard Kris sing at a birthday party. The song, which invites audience participation, appears in Demeanor's 2004 *Party All Night: Kris Demeanor and His Crack Band Live at Ironwood* (Best Before Records). The line "Like the guitar/without the strings" is actually quoted from the song; all the others in the poem are Emma's own.

"The Room:" The "slave castle" is Elmira. Along with Cape Coast Castle, it served as the European base for the world-spanning trade in human beings. From the mid-1600s to the mid-19th Century, millions of Africans were brought to these fortresses and sold from them into forced labour and death. At the castle I discovered that the United Nations had designated Elmira as a World Heritage Site. I now understand this to say that no matter who you are, you cannot understand the world or your place in it without knowing of this place and what it means.

Re: "Saddamandias": In my quest to parody "Ozymandias" in such a way that the poem's imperial assumption could be turned on its head with the poem's own words, I found that the more I worked with Shelley's poem, the more intricate, beautiful and in its own way subversive of the sonnet form I saw it was. I've known the poem a long time. My father and I have it from memory together; it's part of our shared speech. For him, though, I think the poem is most compelling as the voice of the empire he knew and served recognizing both its grandeur and its mortality in the fall of its ancient predecessor. For me, now, the poem has become the sign of how thinking of the grandeur of history is a way of not understanding its human price. Yet I loved the poem at the start of my work with it, and even as I turned it inside out, I found myself loving it only more the more intimately I had to know it by the end.

Cardinal Newman's sentence in "Prayer" is taken from Discourse II, section 7, and quoted by William James in *The Varieties of Religious Experience,* Random House (under The Modern Library imprint), New York, 1999, page 474.

Re: "Brought to You Live," "The Room" and other poems of this kind in this collection: There are two poets who have influenced me in great and particular ways over the years, and who have helped shape my sense of what the poem ought to be: Patrick Lane, with his burden in the horrific and the need to carrying it in art, and di brandt, with her fighting love for the world, and for us.

Though neither has worked with me on this book, each has given me an approach and a language, in person and in their writng, to reach into as much truth about life as my words could handle – and then reach further. To them, my thanks.

The poet referred to in "Envoi" is Susan Glickman; the poem that the italicized line is based on appears in "Winter Solstice" from her 1983 book, *Complicity*, (Signal Editions of Véhicule Press)

ACKNOWLEDGEMENTS

I owe much of this book to the compelling and often risky discussions, to the personal and material support, and to the editorial advice (sometimes all three) that have so generously been given by the following people. To Lisa Rouleau, Rajinderpal S. Pal, Betsy Struthers, Sabrina Reed and Steven Engler, to Dionne Brand, Barry Dempster, Larissa Lai, Paulo da Costa, Gilles Mossière, Antoine Sassine, Maria Jacobs and Noelle Allen, to Isabel Henniger, and to The Thursday Night Group of poets, my thanks for all the time, thought, care and faith you have put into these words. To the Faculty Leave Committee at Mount Royal College, my thanks for approving the sabbatical year during which I was able to do much of the heavy lifting. To my colleagues in the Department of English and my students in Creative Writing, my thanks for helping erase the line between my job and my work. To my wife, Lisa Rouleau, and my children, Emma and Keeghan, my thanks for continuing to astonish me with the meaning of love. And to my parents, Ralph and Doreen Harrison, the thanks of a lifetime.

Richard Harrison is the author of five books of poetry including *Hero of the Play: 10th Anniversary Edition*, and *Big Breath of a Wish* which won the City of Calgary/W.O. Mitchell Book Prize and was a finalist for the Governor-General's Award for Poetry in 1999. His poems have been translated into French, Spanish, Portuguese and Arabic. Richard Harrison has read widely in Canada and the United States and his work has been featured on many TV and radio broadcasts including *Adrienne Clarkson Presents* and Peter Gzowski's *Morningside*. His essays, as well as writing on his work, have appeared in several academic publications as well as in *The Globe and Mail*, *The Manchester Guardian* and *The New York Times*. He lives in Calgary with his wife Lisa and their children, Emma and Keeghan, and he teaches English and Creative Writing at Mount Royal College.

Praise for Richard Harrison's Works

"Richard Harrison's *Hero of the Play* must be the quintessential Canadian Poetry book: it takes a loving though analytic look at the national sport, limning the author's fascination with hockey and with the model of masculinity it offers."　　　– *University of Toronto Quarterly*, 1994

Big Breath of a Wish is superb poetry, emotionally and intellectually packed, visceral verse with a flawless sense of pacing propelled by a confident sense of language.　　　– Gilbert Bouchard, *The Edmonton Journal*, 1999